Zoom In on
Natural Disasters

Tornadoes

Andrea Rivera

abdopublishing.com

Published by Abdo Zoom™, PO Box 398166, Minneapolis, Minnesota 55439. Copyright © 2018 by Abdo Consulting Group, Inc. International copyrights reserved in all countries. No part of this book may be reproduced in any form without written permission from the publisher. Abdo Zoom™ is a trademark and logo of Abdo Consulting Group, Inc.

Printed in the United States of America, North Mankato, Minnesota
022017
092017

**THIS BOOK CONTAINS
RECYCLED MATERIALS**

Cover Photo: Cultura RM Exclusive/Jason Persoff Stormdoctor/Getty Images
Interior Photos: Cultura RM Exclusive/Jason Persoff Stormdoctor/Getty Images, 1; Minerva Studio/ Shutterstock Images, 4; Pete Draper/iStockphoto, 5; Antony Spencer/iStockphoto, 6–7; Melanie Metz/ Shutterstock Images, 7; iStockphoto, 8–9, 14–15; Sue Ogrocki/AP Images, 10; Gibson Ridge Radar/ National Weather Service, 11; Richard A. McMillin/Shutterstock Images, 12; Bob McMillan/FEMA News Photo, 13; Troy & Alesia Cox of Rowlett Texas, 15; NWS/Aberdeen WSFO, 17; Alonzo Adams/AP Images, 18; Clint Spencer/ iStockphoto, 21

Editor: Brienna Rossiter
Series Designer: Madeline Berger
Art Direction: Dorothy Toth

Publisher's Cataloging-in-Publication Data
Names: Rivera, Andrea, author.
Title: Tornadoes / by Andrea Rivera.
Description: Minneapolis, MN : Abdo Zoom, 2018. | Series: Natural disasters |
    Includes bibliographical references and index.
Identifiers: LCCN 2017930339 | ISBN 9781532120398 (lib. bdg.) |
    ISBN 9781614797500 (ebook) | ISBN 9781614798064 (Read-to-me ebook)
Subjects: LCSH: Tornadoes--Juvenile literature.
Classification: DDC 363.34/923--dc23
LC record available at http://lccn.loc.gov/2017930339

Table of Contents

Tornadoes are strong,
spinning winds.

They suck up
everything in their path.

Tornadoes form in **thunderclouds**. Wind makes air in the cloud spin. This forms a **funnel cloud**.

The funnel gets longer. If it touches the ground, it is a tornado.

Technology

Doppler radar tracks storms. It helps scientists predict tornadoes.

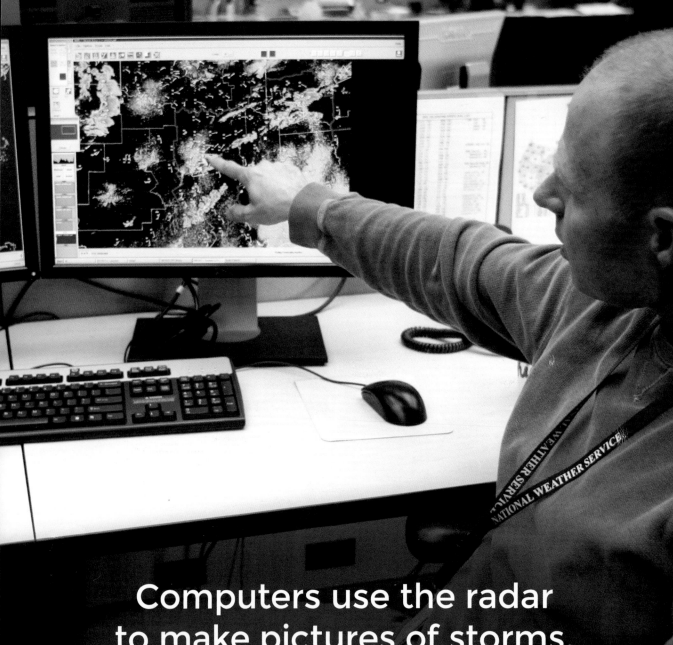

Computers use the radar
to make pictures of storms.

Scientists look for fishhook shapes in the pictures. This shows where tornadoes might form.

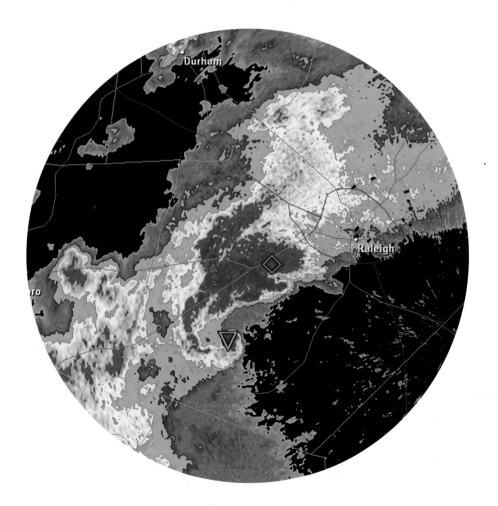

Storm shelters keep people safe during tornadoes.

The shelters are underground. Their walls are thick. There are no windows. This protects people from **debris**.

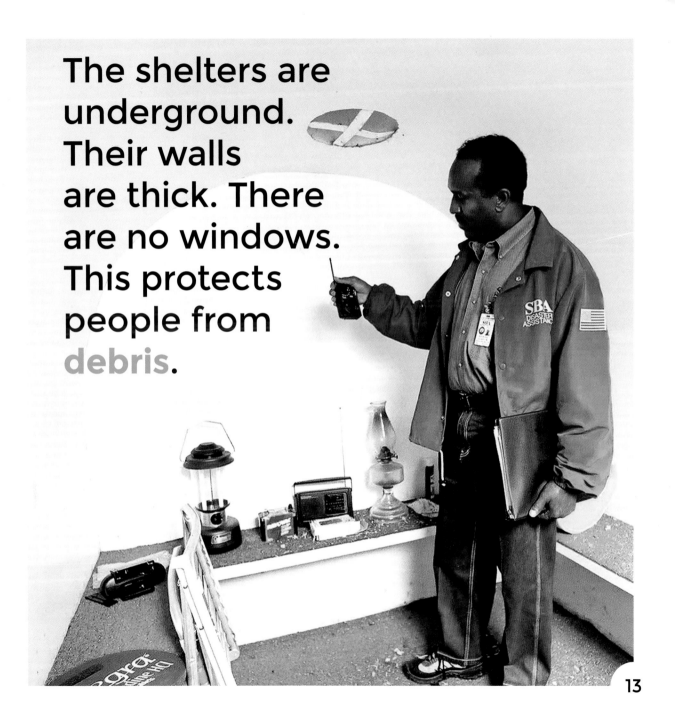

Art

Troy Cox is an artist.
A tornado hit his hometown.
It damaged many houses.

Cox used the debris to make art. He sold the art. He used the money to help people rebuild.

Math

The EF-Scale rates a tornado's strength. EF-0s are weakest. Their wind goes 65 to 85 miles per hour (105 to 137 kmh).

EF-5s are strongest. Their wind is much faster. It goes more than 200 miles per hour (322 kmh).

- A tornado usually lasts about ten minutes.

- Most tornadoes are about 1,600 feet (500 m) wide. Some are more than one mile (1.6 km) wide.

- Most tornadoes have winds that go 100 miles per hour (161 kmh).

- The fastest tornado that has ever been measured had wind speeds of 318 miles per hour (512 kmh).

Glossary

debris - pieces left behind by something that is broken.

Doppler radar - a tool used to track storms and predict the weather.

funnel cloud - a cone-shaped cloud that sticks out from the bottom of a thundercloud.

predict - to guess what might happen in the future.

thundercloud - a huge, dark cloud that can cause storms.

Booklinks

For more information on tornadoes, please visit abdobooklinks.com

 In on STEAM!

Learn even more with the Abdo Zoom STEAM database. Check out abdozoom.com for more information.

Index